I Am 6 and Wonderful

15 Inspiring Short Stories About Courage, Self-Love, Friendship, & Overcoming Fear in Just 5 Minutes a Day

By

Sati Siroda

Book Ecke

I Am 6 and Wonderful

15 Inspiring Short Stories About Courage, Self-Love, Friendship, & Overcoming Fear in Just 5 Minutes a Day

By

Sati Siroda

ISBN

eBook: 978-81-985337-6-0

Paperback: 978-81-985337-0-8

Hardback: 978-81-985337-8-4

First Edition [2025]

Revised [April 2026]

Published by Book Ecke

15A, 4th Floor, City Vista, Tower A,

Suite No.1140, Fountain Road, Kharadi, Pune - 411014

Visit www.bookecke.com for any further information.

To every amazing 6-year-old girl—shine bright, dream big, be kind, believe in yourself, and always know you are truly wonderful! 💖✨

... and Thank You, Charlie Piper!

Table of Contents

Your Free Gift

Hi there, Rockstar! ⭐

I have a special surprise just for you—not one, but **TWO** incredible e-books to make your day even brighter! These free gifts are packed with fun, creativity, and inspiration:

1. **Penguin Coloring Book with Fun Facts**

Get ready for:

- Gorgeous animal illustrations to bring to life with your favorite colors.
- Fascinating fun facts about penguins to learn as you color!

2. **Unstoppable You: 10 Inspiring Stories for Young Achievers**

Jump into:

- 10 best tales that inspire imagination and curiosity.
- Adventures with lessons and empowering affirmations!

Just ask your awesome grown-up to scan the QR code to grab your free e-books!

Scan Me

Introduction

Heya, Wonderful Girl! 💖

What's up?

Did you know that you are strong, smart, and full of magic? That's right—YOU! Sometimes, you might feel a little shy or unsure, and that's okay. Even the bravest girls feel that way. But always remember—inside you is a heart full of courage and a mind full of dreams!

This Book Is Just for You! 📖

I wrote this book because I believe in YOU! These little stories will remind you how special you are and help you feel even more confident, kind, and proud of yourself. When I was little, I sometimes felt sad too, but stories helped me believe in myself. Now, I hope these stories do the same for you!

Why You'll Love This Book! 💕

Hey, wonderful you! Want to know why this book is extra special? Let me tell you!

- The stories are short and super fun—perfect for a quick break (or a bedtime story!).
- Each story has a little secret—a special lesson to help you feel stronger, braver, and more confident.
- After every story, there's a fun affirmation to remind you just how amazing you are, plus cool activities to try!
- And the best part? This book is all about YOU—helping you be your happiest, most wonderful self!

Are You Ready? 🚀

Let's go on an adventure together! Every page is filled with fun stories that will make you smile, think, and feel extra proud of yourself. So, snuggle up, open your heart, and let's begin!

Because, my dear, you are **6 and WONDERFUL! 💖**

With love and big hugs,

Sati

Part 1: Every Big Thing Starts Small

Heya, Brave Explorer!

Have you ever wanted to try something new but felt a little unsure? Maybe it was your first time riding a bike, learning to swim, or even speaking up in front of a group. It can feel a little scary, right? That's okay! Everyone feels that way sometimes.

But here's a little secret—every big thing starts small. Every amazing dancer once took their very first shaky step. Every artist once held a crayon for the first time. Every great adventure began with just one tiny moment of courage.

In this chapter, you'll meet someone who had to take that first step, even when they weren't sure what would happen next. By the time you finish these stories in Part-1, you'll see that being brave isn't about never feeling scared—it's about trying anyway.

So, are you ready to start your own big adventure? Let's go!

Chapter 1: Kaia and the Bicycle Fall

Kaia had been waiting for this day forever. Today, she was finally going to ride her big-girl bicycle without training wheels! Her pink bike with shiny streamers was ready. Her helmet was snug on her head. And her dad was standing right beside her, smiling proudly.

"You can do this, Kaia," her dad said, holding onto the back of her bike. "Just pedal and keep your balance."

Kaia took a deep breath, placed her feet on the pedals, and gripped the handlebars tightly. This was it—she was ready!

Dad gave her a gentle push, and Kaia started pedaling. The cool breeze brushed against her cheeks as she moved forward. "I'm doing it!" she squealed. "I'm really doing it!"

But then—uh-oh! The bike wobbled. Kaia's heart pounded. She tried to steady herself, but it was too late.

CRASH!

She tumbled onto the grass, scraping her knee.

"Ow…" Kaia sniffled, looking at her knee. A tiny tear formed in her eye. The ground felt hard, and her knee stung. Maybe riding without training wheels wasn't such a good idea after all.

Dad rushed over and knelt beside her. "Are you okay, sweet pea?" he asked gently, brushing some dirt off her knee.

Kaia nodded slowly, but she felt unsure inside. What if she fell again? What if she never learned to ride?

Kaia's best friend, Mia, came running over. "Kaia, that was a great first try!" she said with a big smile. "You almost had it!"

Kaia frowned. "But I fell."

Mia nodded. "Yeah, but everybody falls! Remember when I was learning to swim? I was so scared to put my face in the water, but I kept trying. Now I can swim all the way across the pool!"

Kaia thought about that. Mia had been scared, but she didn't give up. Maybe she could be brave too.

Dad smiled. "Kaia, being brave doesn't mean you won't fall. It means that even when you do, you stand back up, take a deep breath, and try again. Every time you get back on your bike, you are learning, growing, and becoming stronger."

Kaia wiped her tears and took a deep breath. "Okay," she said. "I'll try again."

Dad helped her stand up, and Mia held her hand for a moment. "It's okay to be scared," Mia said. "But you're already braver than you think. The first time is always the hardest."

Kaia looked at her bike. It seemed a little scarier than before, but she remembered how much fun it felt when she had pedaled on her own, even for a few seconds.

"What if I fall again?" she asked.

"Then we help you up, and you try again," Dad said smiling. "Each time, you'll get better and stronger."

Kaia looked at Mia, who nodded encouragingly. She thought about how proud she would feel if she could finally ride on her own. She didn't want to quit now.

She nodded firmly. "Okay. Let's do this."

Kaia climbed back onto her bike. Her hands felt a little shaky, but she was determined. "Hold on, Daddy!" she said.

"I've got you," Dad said, steadying the bike. "Now, count to three and start pedaling."

Kaia counted. "One… two… three!"

She pushed off, pedaling faster and faster. Her bike wobbled, but she kept going.

"I'm doing it!" she shouted, giggling. "Look, Mia!"

Dad let go, and Kaia kept riding all by herself! She zoomed down the sidewalk, her hair flying behind her. The whole world felt exciting and free!

"I did it! I really did it! Yay!" Kaia cheered.

Mia and Dad clapped and cheered. "You did it, Kaia!"

Kaia came to a stop, hopping off her bike. She looked at her scraped knee and smiled. "I'm glad I tried again," she said proudly.

Dad gave her a hug. "That's my brave girl."

What Kaia Learned

Kaia learned that being brave didn't mean never falling—it meant getting back up after she did. She realized that every time she tried, she got better and stronger. And most importantly, she learned that courage isn't about being perfect—it's about never giving up.

Affirmation for Courage

Write this affirmation in your notebook and say it whenever you feel scared:

"I am strong, I am brave, and I always get back up!"

Try This

- Think of something that scares you a little—like climbing the jungle gym or learning a new skill. Try it, even if it feels tricky at first!
- The next time you fall or make a mistake, instead of giving up, take a deep breath and say, "I'll try again."
- Encourage a friend to be brave too! Remind them that mistakes are part of learning.

Kaia's story reminds us that falling isn't failing—it's just part of the ride. What will you be brave enough to try today?

Chapter 2: Freya's First Day of School

Freya clutched her backpack straps tightly as she stood before her new school. The big red doors looked taller than she had imagined, and the children running around the playground seemed to know each other already. Her tummy felt like it was full of fluttering butterflies.

"I don't want to go," she whispered, holding onto her mom's hand.

Her mom knelt beside her. "It's okay to be nervous, sweetheart. But remember, every new adventure starts with a little bit of bravery."

Freya wasn't sure if she had enough bravery for today.

The school bell rang, and children started walking inside. Freya took a deep breath and shuffled forward. As soon as she stepped into the bright, colorful classroom, her heart pounded even faster. What if she didn't make any friends? What if she got lost? What if she missed her mom too much?

"Good morning, Freya!" said a warm, friendly voice.

Freya looked up and saw her teacher, Miss Lily, smiling at her. "We're so happy you're here. Come find your cubby and take a seat with the other children."

Freya gulped. "Okay…" she said softly.

She found a cubby with her name on it and slowly put her backpack inside. She glanced around the room. Some kids were already talking and laughing. Others were coloring at their desks. Freya took another deep breath and sat at an empty table.

Miss Lily clapped her hands. "Let's start with something fun! I want everyone to share their name and their favorite thing to do."

Freya felt her hands get sweaty. What if her voice came out too soft? What if she said the wrong thing? Her turn was getting closer. Five kids left. Four. Three. Two.

Then Miss Lily smiled at her. "Your turn, Freya!"

She could feel her heart thumping. But then she remembered what her mom had said—every adventure starts with bravery. She took a deep breath, sat up straight, and said, "My name is Freya, and I love to paint pictures of animals."

Miss Lily beamed. "That's wonderful, Freya! I bet you'll love art class."

The girl next to her, Ava, turned and grinned. "I like to paint too! Maybe we can sit together in art class."

Freya's tummy butterflies felt a little smaller. "Okay!" she said, smiling back.

Throughout the day, Freya kept trying little things, even when she felt nervous. She raised her hand when Miss Lily asked a question, even though her voice was a little shaky. She asked another girl where the bathroom was and thanked her with a small smile. At lunchtime, she hesitated before getting in line, but then she saw Ava waving her over. "Come stand with me!" Ava said, and Freya felt a warm feeling spread inside her. She lined up with the other kids without looking back for her mom.

Each time, the fear got a little smaller. Each time, she felt a little braver.

By recess, she was playing on the swings with Ava and another girl named Sofia. Ava told Freya about her cat named Whiskers, and Freya giggled at the silly stories. They laughed and raced each other to the jungle gym, cheering as they climbed to the top. "You're really fast!" Ava said. "Maybe tomorrow we can play tag!" Freya grinned and nodded. She had almost forgotten how scared she had been that morning.

What Freya Learned

By the end of the day, Freya realized something amazing—trying, even when she was scared, helped her feel stronger. She had made new friends, learned where everything was, and had fun! She still missed her mom, but she knew she would see her soon. Most importantly, she had proved to herself that she *could* be brave.

Affirmation for Bravery

Write this affirmation in your notebook and say it whenever you feel nervous:

"I have the courage to try, the strength to learn, and the heart to keep going!"

Try This

- Sit with a friend or family member and take turns sharing a time when you felt nervous but tried something new anyway. Talk about what happened and how you felt afterward.
- Ask someone you trust about a time they had to be brave. Listen to their story and think about what you can learn from their experience.
- Make a list of new things you want to try, like a new activity, food, or hobby. Pick one and share your experience with someone!

Freya's story reminds us that new things can feel scary at first, but with courage, we can turn them into amazing adventures. What will you be brave enough to try today?

Chapter 3: Emiko and the Playground Bullies

Emiko loved the playground. She loved swinging high into the sky, climbing the jungle gym, and sliding down the biggest slide. But today, the playground didn't feel fun. Today, Emiko felt small and scared.

It all started when a group of older girls wouldn't let her play.

"You can't go on the swings," one of them said, crossing her arms. "These are for us."

Emiko's heart sank. "But there are so many swings," she whispered.

"Didn't you hear me?" another girl said, stepping closer. "Go away."

Tears filled Emiko's eyes as she turned and ran to a quiet corner of the playground. She wanted to tell someone, but she was too scared. What if they laughed at her? What if they got even meaner? She stayed silent all day, her heart heavy.

That evening, Emiko's dad noticed she wasn't her usual bubbly self. "What's wrong, sweetheart?" he asked gently.

Emiko hesitated. Then, in a small voice, she told him everything.

Her dad's face grew serious. He took her hands in his and said, "Emiko, I need you to listen carefully. When someone is mean to you or others, that's not okay. That's called bullying. And it's not just about you—it's about making sure no one else gets hurt too."

Emiko wiped her tears. "But what if they don't stop?"

Her dad squeezed her hands. "That's why you have to tell your teacher. Bullying doesn't stop when we stay silent. It stops when we stand up for ourselves and for others."

Emiko sniffled. "But I'm scared."

"That's okay," her dad said. "Being brave doesn't mean you're not scared. It means you do the right thing even when you are."

Emiko thought about that all night. Could she really be brave enough to speak up?

The next morning, Emiko walked to school with her dad's words in her heart. As she reached the playground, she saw something that made her stop.

The same group of girls was blocking another girl, Hana, from getting on the slide. Hana's face looked just like Emiko's had the day before—sad and scared.

Something inside Emiko sparked. She remembered what her dad had said. *It's not just about me. It's about protecting others too.*

She took a deep breath, her hands trembling, and marched up to the bullies.

"That's not fair," she said firmly. "The playground is for everyone."

The tallest girl rolled her eyes. "And what are you going to do about it?"

"I'm going to tell the teacher," Emiko said, standing tall. "Because bullying is wrong."

The girls stared at her. Then, one by one, they stepped back. They muttered something and walked away, leaving Hana standing there, eyes wide.

"Thank you, Emiko," Hana whispered.

Emiko smiled. "Do you want to go on the slide together?"

Hana grinned. "Yes!"

Emiko didn't stop there. After recess, she told her teacher what had happened. Miss Yuki listened carefully and nodded. "You did the right thing, Emiko. And because of your courage, we can make sure the playground is safe for everyone."

Over the next few weeks, something amazing happened. The bullies stopped pushing kids away. More children felt safe playing. And Emiko? She felt stronger than ever.

One afternoon, the tallest bully—her name was Aiko—came up to Emiko and looked at the ground. "I… I'm sorry," she mumbled. "We didn't think we were hurting anyone."

Emiko smiled. "It's okay. Maybe next time, we can all play together."

Aiko looked surprised but nodded. "Yeah… I'd like that."

What Emiko Learned

Emiko learned that courage isn't about being fearless—it's about doing the right thing, even when you're scared. She discovered that standing up to bullies doesn't just help you, it helps others too. And most of all, she saw that kindness has the power to change even the meanest hearts.

Affirmation for Courage

Write this affirmation in your notebook and say it whenever you feel scared:

“I have the courage to speak up, the strength to stand tall, and the kindness to make a difference.”

Try This

- Practice using a strong, determined voice when you speak. It helps you feel more confident!
- Think of someone you admire who stands up for others. What makes them brave? How can you be like them?
- Role-play with a friend or family member about what to do if you see someone being treated unfairly. Talking about it helps you be ready in real life!

Emiko’s story reminds us that one brave voice can make a big difference. Who will you stand up for today?

Part 2: The Magic of Believing in Yourself

Heya, Little Star!

Have you ever looked in the mirror and wished you could be a little different? Maybe you thought, *I wish I were faster, smarter, or braver like someone else.* But guess what? You are already wonderful—just the way you are!

Confidence isn't about being the best at everything. It's about believing in yourself—even when things feel tricky or new. It's about knowing that your kindness, your creativity, your ideas, and your smile make the world a brighter place.

In this chapter, you'll meet someone who learns that loving who you are is the first step to feeling confident. By the time you finish these stories, you'll see that the most magical kind of love is the love you give yourself.

So, are you ready to unlock the magic inside you? Let's begin!

Chapter 4: Lucinda and the Dance of Confidence

Lucinda loved dancing. She twirled in the living room, leaped across the playground, and tapped her feet to music wherever she went. But today, as she stood in her dance class, her excitement melted into worry.

Her teacher, Miss Clara, clapped her hands. “Today, we are learning a brand-new dance move! It’s called the spin-jump.”

Lucinda’s stomach flipped. A *spin-jump*? That sounded tricky.

Miss Clara demonstrated, gracefully spinning on one foot before jumping into the air and landing softly. The other students clapped with excitement.

Lucinda gulped. *I can’t do that!* Her feet suddenly felt heavy, and her hands clenched into little fists. What if she tripped? What if everyone laughed at her?

The students tried the spin-jump one by one. Some wobbled, some landed perfectly, and others giggled as they tried again. Then, it was Lucinda’s turn.

She took a deep breath, bent her knees, and spun. But when she jumped, her foot slipped, and she landed on the floor with a soft *thud*.

Giggles filled the room. Lucinda's cheeks burned. She quickly scrambled to her feet, but her heart felt heavy. *I knew it. I can't do this.*

Miss Clara knelt beside her. "Lucinda, are you okay?"

Lucinda nodded, but her lip trembled. "I can't do it," she whispered.

Miss Clara smiled kindly. "Not yet. But you *can* learn."

Lucinda frowned. "But what if I never get it right?"

Miss Clara sat beside her. "Let me tell you a secret, Lucinda. Confidence isn't about being the best. It's about believing you can improve. The more you try, the stronger you get."

Lucinda sniffled. "Even if I fall again?"

Miss Clara nodded. "Especially if you fall again. Every fall is just another step toward getting better."

Lucinda thought about that as she watched the other girls practice. Some of them were still stumbling, but they laughed and tried again. She saw Evelyn, one of her classmates, trip over her own feet and burst into giggles before hopping up and trying again. Another girl, Maria, landed perfectly but then wobbled and almost fell.

They're not afraid to keep going, Lucinda realized. *Maybe I should try again too.*

She took a deep breath and stood up. This time, she focused on what Miss Clara had said. She bent her knees, spun carefully, and jumped. She landed with a little wobble but stayed on her feet! It wasn't perfect, but it was better than before.

Miss Clara clapped. "That was much better, Lucinda! See? You're improving already."

Lucinda felt a tiny spark of confidence light up inside her. She wasn't perfect yet, but maybe, just maybe, she *could* get there.

Lucinda thought about that as she watched the other girls practice. Some of them were still stumbling, but they laughed and tried again.

Maybe I should try again too, she thought.

She took a deep breath and stood up. This time, she focused on what Miss Clara had said. She bent her knees, spun carefully, and jumped. She landed with a little wobble but stayed on her feet!

Miss Clara clapped. "That was much better, Lucinda!"

Lucinda smiled. It wasn't perfect, but it was progress.

That evening, Lucinda couldn't stop thinking about the spin-jump. She wanted to get better. So, after dinner, she stood in front of the mirror in her bedroom and tried again. She spun, jumped, and landed with a small stumble. She tried again. And again. Each time, she got a little steadier, a little stronger.

The next morning, she practiced in the backyard while her mom watched from the porch. "That looks great, sweetheart!" her mom encouraged.

At the grocery store, while waiting in line with her dad, Lucinda balanced on one foot and imagined the movement in her head. When no one was looking, she did a tiny spin. Her dad chuckled, "Thinking about dance, huh?"

Lucinda nodded. She had never thought about practicing like this before. It didn't have to be just in class—she could keep getting better anywhere!

At the next dance class, Miss Clara asked if anyone wanted to demonstrate the spin-jump. Lucinda's heart raced. Could she really do it in front of everyone?

She took a deep breath and raised her hand. "I'll try."

"Go ahead, Lucinda!" Miss Clara encouraged.

Lucinda stepped forward. She bent her knees, spun, and jumped. And this time—she landed perfectly! No wobbling, no falling—just a smooth, graceful landing.

The whole class cheered.

Lucinda grinned from ear to ear. She had done it! No because she was the best, but because she believed in herself and kept trying. And that, she realized, was what confidence truly meant.

What Lucinda Learned

Lucinda learned that confidence isn't just about getting things right the first time; it's about trusting yourself and understanding that practice makes you stronger. She realized that mistakes aren't failures—they're steps toward success.

Affirmation for Inner Strength

Write this affirmation in your notebook and say it whenever you feel like giving up:

"I am strong, I am learning, and I believe in myself."

Try This

- Think of something you struggled with but kept practicing. How did you improve? Share your story with a friend or family member.
- Practice a new skill every day, even if it feels tricky at first. Keep a little note of your progress.
- Encourage a friend when they feel like saying, "I can't." Remind them that learning takes time!

Lucinda's story shows us that confidence grows when we believe in ourselves and keep trying. What will you practice today?

Chapter 5: Paloma's Big Moment

Paloma loved playing dress-up with her mom. She twirled in pretty skirts, giggled in fluffy coats, and loved the way her shoes made little tapping sounds on the floor. But when it came to dressing herself, Paloma didn't feel so sure.

Every morning, her mom helped button her coat, tie her shoes, and zip up her dress. And every morning, Paloma wished she could do it on her own. But whenever she tried, the buttons slipped, the zipper got stuck, and the shoelaces turned into messy knots.

"I can't do it," she would sigh, letting her mom take over.

One chilly morning, as Paloma sat on her bed staring at her coat, she decided something. *I want to do this by myself.*

As her mom helped her with her socks, Paloma hesitated. "Mom," she said softly. "Can I try dressing myself today?"

Mom's eyes twinkled. "Of course, sweetheart. But let's talk about something important first."

She sat beside Paloma and took her hand. "Dressing yourself is part of growing up, and that also means learning about body boundaries. No one should ever touch you in a way that makes you uncomfortable, even when helping you dress."

Paloma's eyes widened. "Not even friends?"

Mom gave her a reassuring smile. "Not even friends. If something doesn't feel right, you have the right to say no and tell a grown-up you trust. Your feelings are important, and your voice matters."

Paloma thought about this for a moment. It felt a little scary to talk about, but she understood. She knew that sometimes things felt okay, and sometimes they didn't. Now she knew she could always speak up.

"What if I get nervous?" Paloma asked.

Mom squeezed her hand. "Then you take a deep breath and remember that you are in charge of yourself. You are strong and smart, and if you need help, you can always talk to me or another safe adult."

Paloma thought about this for a moment. It felt a little scary to talk about, but she understood. "Okay," she said, feeling a little braver. "I'll remember."

Mom smiled. "Good. Now, let's get you dressed!"

Paloma grabbed her favorite pink coat and held it up. "Okay, I can do this."

She stuck one arm in, then the other. So far, so good. But then came the tricky part—the buttons.

Her fingers fumbled, trying to slip the tiny buttons through the little holes. They just wouldn't go in! Frustration bubbled inside her.

"Ugh! This is too hard!" she huffed.

Her mom knelt beside her. "It's okay, sweetie. Try again. Take a deep breath and go slow."

Paloma took a deep breath and tried again. This time, she got the first button through! A big smile spread across her face. "I did it!"

Her mom clapped. "See? You're learning already."

Now for the hardest part—her shoes.

Paloma stared at her shoelaces. No matter how hard she tried, they always twisted and tangled. She took a deep breath and started looping one lace over the other, just like her mom had shown her. She stuck her tongue out slightly, concentrating as hard as she could.

She made a loop, wrapped the other lace around, and… *oh no!* The bow slipped loose. The laces flopped apart, and her hands dropped to her sides.

Paloma groaned. "I'll never get it right."

Her mom sat beside her and gently placed a hand on her shoulder. "Remember what we talked about? Learning something new takes time. Instead of saying 'I can't,' try saying 'I'm learning.'"

Paloma frowned. "I'm learning…" she whispered. "I'm learning, and I will keep trying."

She picked up the laces again and tried once more. Loop, wrap, pull—this time, the bow almost stayed in place, but one lace was much longer than the other. She sighed but didn't give up.

Paloma took another deep breath and slowed even further. She carefully looped the lace, wrapped the other one around her, and gently pulled it tight.

The bow stayed! It wasn't perfect, but it was tied!

Paloma gasped. "Mom, look! I did it!"

Her mom beamed. "I knew you could! And you kept trying even when it was hard. That's what makes you strong."

Paloma wiggled her toes inside her shoes. They felt different now—not just because she had tied them herself, but because she had done something she thought she couldn't.

She ran to the mirror and twirled. "I dressed myself!" she said proudly, spinning on her tiptoes. She stretched out her arms, looking at her buttoned coat, and then bent down to admire her laces. They weren't the neatest bows, but they were *hers*.

Paloma beamed. "At first, I thought I couldn't do it," she said, her hands on her hips. "But I just had to keep trying."

Mom knelt beside her, brushing a strand of hair from her face. "That's the most important lesson, sweetheart. Strength isn't about getting everything right the first time—it's about believing in yourself and not giving up."

Paloma giggled and gave her mom a tight hug. "I feel strong, like a big kid now."

Mom kissed the top of her head. "You *are* a big kid, Paloma. And you can do anything you set your mind to."

As Paloma walked out the door, she bounced on her feet, feeling the bows on her shoes with every step.

What Paloma Learned

Paloma learned that growing up means believing in herself and trying new things, even when they feel hard at first. She discovered that small steps lead to big victories and that her voice and body belong to her.

Affirmation for Strength and Confidence

Write this affirmation in your notebook and say it whenever you need a boost:

"I am strong, I am learning, and I believe in myself."

Try This

- Try dressing yourself differently for the next few days. Even if it takes time, keep practicing!
- Make a list of things you're learning to do on your own and check them off as you master them.
- Talk to a trusted adult about body boundaries and practice saying, "No, I don't like that," in a strong voice.

Paloma's story shows us that every small step makes us stronger. What new thing will *you* try today?

Chapter 6: Stella and the Slippery Path

Stella loved riding her bike. After finishing her homework every afternoon, she would put on her helmet, hop on her shiny blue bicycle, and zoom around the neighborhood. She loved the feeling of the wind in her hair and the sound of her wheels whirring against the pavement.

But today was different.

Dark clouds covered the sky, and raindrops pitter-pattered on the ground. Stella sat by the window, watching puddles form on the sidewalk.

"Maybe I shouldn't ride today," she mumbled, feeling unsure.

Her mom smiled. "A little rain is okay, but you have to be extra careful. Remember, when things get tricky, stay steady and trust yourself."

Stella nodded, repeating her mom's words in her mind. *Stay steady and trust myself.* She took a deep breath, grabbed her raincoat, and headed outside.

Stella swung her leg over her bike and placed her feet on the pedals. The cool air brushed against her face as she started to ride. She loved the way the rain smelled—fresh and clean, like the whole world had just woken up.

As she reached the park, she saw a giant puddle in the middle of the path. Stella's heart started to race. The ground looked wet and slippery. What if she lost control? What if she fell?

She thought about turning back, but then she remembered what her mom had told her. *Stay steady and trust yourself.*

"I can do this," she whispered.

She gripped the handlebars tighter and slowed down. Taking a deep breath, she carefully pedaled through the puddle, keeping her body balanced.

SPLASH!

Water sprayed everywhere, but Stella kept her focus. Her bike wobbled slightly, but she didn't panic. She adjusted her balance and kept going.

A few seconds later, she was on the other side.

She did it!

Stella stopped her bike and looked back at the puddle. A big smile spread across her face. "I almost slipped, but I stayed calm!" she said proudly.

She realized something important—handling unexpected situations wasn't about avoiding them. It was about trusting herself, staying focused, and pushing through.

Just then, her best friend, Lila, rode up beside her. "Wow, Stella! You went right through that puddle! Weren't you scared?"

Stella nodded. "A little. But I told myself I could do it, and I did!"

Lila grinned. "You're so brave! I always get nervous about riding when it's wet."

Stella thought for a moment. "You just have to go slow, keep steady, and believe in yourself."

Lila smiled. "Okay, I'll try!"

Just as Stella was about to move forward, she heard a loud *whoosh!* A gust of wind blew through the trees, sending leaves swirling around them. The sky darkened, and a light drizzle turned into heavier raindrops.

Stella's heart pounded. The path ahead looked slicker now, and a long stretch of puddles covered the road. The thought of her tires skidding made her grip the handlebars tighter.

What if I lose control? What if I fall?

She glanced at Lila, who looked just as nervous. "Maybe we should turn back," Lila said hesitantly.

Stella swallowed her fear and took a deep breath. *No. I can do this. I already rode through one puddle. I just need to go slow and steady.*

She took a cautious step forward and placed her foot back on the pedal. "Let's take it one step at a time," she told Lila. "If we get scared, we'll stop and breathe."

Lila nodded, and together, they started pedaling forward. The rain splattered on Stella's jacket, and her bike wobbled slightly as she hit a bigger puddle. Her heart thumped faster. But she tightened her grip and focused on staying steady.

The wheels slid just a tiny bit, but she adjusted her balance like before. *I've got this,* she told herself.

As they neared the end of the path, Stella felt her confidence growing with every pedal. She wasn't letting fear stop her. She was pushing through it, proving to herself that she was stronger than she thought.

Finally, they reached a dry patch of road. Lila let out a deep breath. "We did it!" she cheered.

Stella laughed, feeling a rush of pride. "See? We stayed calm and made it through!"

Lila high-fived her. "You were right! That wasn't so bad!"

As the rain started to slow, Stella looked back at the path they had conquered. It had been scary, but she had faced it, and now she felt unstoppable.

That night, Stella thought about what had happened. Instead of giving up, she had faced her fear and made it through. She wanted to remember this feeling.

She grabbed a small piece of paper and wrote: **"I rode through a puddle and stayed calm!"** Then, she folded the note and put it in a little jar on her desk.

Her mom peeked into the room. "What are you doing, sweetheart?"

Stella held up the jar. "I'm starting a success jar! Whenever I do something that makes me feel proud, I'll write it down and keep it here."

Her mom smiled. "That's a wonderful idea!"

Stella nodded. She already felt stronger just thinking about it.

What Stella Learned

Stella learned that challenges can be scary, but staying calm and believing in herself helps her push through. She realized that confidence grows with every little success, and keeping track of those moments makes her feel even stronger.

Affirmation for Self-Belief

Write this affirmation in your notebook and say it whenever you feel unsure:

"I trust myself, I stay calm, and I can handle anything."

Try This

- Start a success jar like Stella! Write down moments when you feel proud and keep them in a special place.
- Think of a time when you were nervous but did something anyway. Share your story with a friend or family member and ask them about a time they were brave too!

- Play a confidence game! Take turns with a friend or family member saying one thing you like about yourself. Keep going until you both run out of ideas!

Stella's story reminds us that even the trickiest moments can be overcome with confidence and trust. What challenge will you face today?

Part 3: The Magic of Friendship

Heya, Sweet Little Girl!

Have you ever had a friend who made you smile on a sad day? Or maybe you've been that friend for someone else! Friendship isn't just about playing together—it's about kindness, laughter, and always being there for each other.

The best friendships aren't about being the same or always agreeing. They're about understanding, sharing, and making each other feel special. A true friend listens, helps, and makes the world a little brighter just by being in it.

By the time you finish these stories, you'll see that being a good friend doesn't just make others happy—it makes you stronger too!

So, are you ready to discover the magic of friendship? Let's get started!

Chapter 7: Liana and the Language Bridge

Liana loved making new friends. She loved playing hopscotch at recess, sharing her crayons in class, and giggling with her best friend, Sonia, during lunch. But one day, someone new joined their class—a girl named Akari.

Akari had just moved from Japan, and she looked nervous as she stood in front of the room. Her hands clutched the straps of her backpack tightly, and her eyes darted around as if she wasn't sure where to go.

"This is Akari," Miss Davis said with a warm smile. "She's new to our school and still learning English. Let's all make her feel welcome."

Liana's heart squeezed a little. She couldn't imagine what it would feel like to be in a brand-new school where no one spoke her language.

She glanced at the other kids. Some whispered to each other, and others nodded politely, but no one walked up to Akari.

Liana took a deep breath. *Maybe I can help.*

During recess, Liana found Akari sitting alone on a bench, looking down at her hands. She was fidgeting with the hem of her sweater, her shoulders slightly hunched. Kids laughed and played all around her, but Akari sat still, watching them with hesitant eyes.

Liana felt a slight flutter of nervousness in her chest. What if Akari didn't understand her? What if she didn't want to talk? But then she thought about how lonely Akari must feel, being in a new place where everything sounded unfamiliar.

Taking a deep breath, Liana walked over slowly, her sneakers crunching on the gravel. She stopped in front of Akari and smiled brightly. "Hi, Akari," she said, trying to make her voice as warm as possible. "I'm Liana."

Akari looked up and blinked. Her eyes were wide, and she hesitated before answering. "H-Hi," she said softly, her voice unsure.

Liana could tell Akari was struggling to find the right words. She remembered what her teacher had said—sometimes, actions spoke louder than words. So, instead of saying more, Liana pointed to herself and repeated, "Liana." Then she pointed gently to Akari with a questioning look.

Akari's eyes lit up in understanding. "Akari!" she said, pressing a hand to her chest.

Liana grinned. That was it! They had just had their first conversation without needing many words at all. She felt a spark of excitement—maybe this was the start of something special.

The next day, Liana sat beside Akari at lunch. She noticed that Akari had a small bento box with neatly packed rice and fish.

Liana pointed at the food and smiled. "Looks yummy!" she said.

Akari tilted her head, then nodded. "Onigiri," she said, pointing to the rice ball.

Liana's eyes widened. "O-ni-gi-ri," she repeated slowly. "I like that word!"

Akari giggled and nodded. Then she pointed at Liana's sandwich. "Bread?" she asked.

Liana nodded. "Yes, sandwich!"

For the rest of lunch, they took turns pointing at things and saying their names. Liana learned that "mizu" meant water, and Akari learned that "friend" meant "tomodachi." They laughed at each other's funny pronunciations, and soon, Akari wasn't looking so nervous anymore.

Over the next few days, Liana started teaching Akari small English words, like "thank you" and "good morning." In return, Akari taught Liana how to count in Japanese.

One afternoon, Miss Davis asked the class a question about animals. Liana saw Akari hesitate, gripping her pencil tightly.

Liana leaned over and whispered, "You can say 'cat.'"

Akari took a deep breath and whispered back, "Neko?"

Liana smiled and nodded. "Yes! Cat is 'neko' in Japanese!"

Miss Davis turned to them. "Would you like to share, Akari?"

Akari looked at Liana, who gave her an encouraging nod. Taking a deep breath, Akari stood up. "Cat is…neko," she said softly. "In English…cat."

The class clapped, and Akari beamed. Liana felt a warm glow inside her chest. She had helped her friend feel included.

One day, Liana found a book about Japan in the library. She saw pictures of cherry blossoms, colorful kimonos, and busy streets in Tokyo.

She ran up to Akari. "I found a book about Japan!" she said excitedly. "Can you tell me more about it?"

Akari's face lit up with happiness. "Yes!" she said. "I'll… show you, my home."

As they flipped through the pages, Akari explained how children in Japan took off their shoes before entering school and neatly placed them in cubbies before changing into indoor slippers. She described how her old classroom had sliding doors and tatami mats, different from the desks and chairs at their current school. Liana listened with wide eyes, imagining what it would be like to walk on soft mats instead of a hard floor.

Akari then pointed to a picture of glowing lanterns floating in the night sky. "This is Tanabata festival," she said excitedly. "We write wishes on colorful papers and hang them on bamboo trees!" She traced the photo with her finger. "Last year, I wished to make new friends."

Liana gasped. "And now you have!" she said, squeezing Akari's hand gently. "That sounds so magical. I want to celebrate Tanabata too!"

Liana leaned forward, her excitement growing. "You know what, Akari? The world is so big, and there are so many amazing things to learn. I think the world is better when we share and learn from each other."

Akari nodded. "Yes. We are tomodachi."

Liana grinned. "And that means 'friends.'"

What Liana Learned

Liana learned that friendship goes beyond words. By listening, learning, and being kind, she had built a bridge between two languages and two cultures. She realized that differences don't separate people—they bring them closer together.

Affirmation for Understanding

Write this affirmation in your notebook and say it whenever you want to connect with someone new:

"I listen, I learn, and I make the world a friendlier place."

Try This

- Find someone who speaks a different language and learn a few words from them. You might teach them something in return!
- Ask a classmate or friend about their favorite family tradition. What makes it special?
- If you see someone feeling left out, invite them to play or talk. A small act of kindness can make a big difference!

Liana's story reminds us that kindness and understanding can turn strangers into friends. Who will you reach out to today?

Chapter 8: Quinn and the Helping Hands

Quinn loved living in the countryside. She loved the vast, open fields, the sound of birds chirping in the morning, and the way the air smelled fresh and sweet. But most of all, she loved playing with her best friend, Jenny. They ran through the meadows, picked apples from the orchard, and sometimes even helped Jenny's grandfather on his farm.

But one day, something was different. Jenny wasn't at their usual meeting spot by the big oak tree. When Quinn finally found her, she was sitting on the fence of her grandfather's farm, her head resting on her arms.

"What's wrong, Jenny?" Quinn asked, climbing up beside her.

Jenny sighed. "The flood ruined our farm," she said softly. "Grandpa says we have to start all over again. There's so much work to do, and I won't have time to play anymore."

Quinn's heart sank. She looked around at the farm. The once-green fields were muddy and messy. Some of the wooden fences had fallen, and parts of the barn roof were missing. It was worse than she had imagined.

She thought for a moment, then smiled. "Jenny, we'll help you! You don't have to do this alone."

Jenny looked up. "But it's so much work. And who would help?"

Quinn jumped off the fence. "Everyone! We'll ask all the kids in the village. If we work together, we can fix the farm and still have time to play!"

That afternoon, Quinn ran from house to house, knocking on doors and telling her friends about Jenny's farm.

"Jenny's farm was ruined by the flood," she told Laura.

"Oh no!" Laura gasped. "How can we help?"

"We can clean up, plant new crops, and fix fences," Quinn said. "If we all work together, it won't take long!"

Laura nodded. "I'll ask my brother too!"

Quinn kept going. She told Noah, Emma, and even the older kids, Jack and Maya. Soon, almost every child in the village had promised to help.

The next morning, a group of kids arrived at Jenny's farm, ready to work. Jenny's eyes widened when she saw them. "You all came?"

Quinn grinned. "Of course! We're friends, and friends help each other."

Jenny's grandfather wiped his eyes. "I never thought I'd see so many helping hands. Thank you, kids."

The children got to work. Some picked up branches and sticks left by the flood. Others helped rebuild the broken fences.

Quinn and Jenny worked together, digging in the rich, brown soil and planting new seeds. "This will be wheat," Jenny said, patting the dirt gently. "And over there, we'll plant carrots."

Jack and Maya carried heavy wooden planks to fix the barn's roof. "This is hard work," Jack huffed, wiping sweat from his forehead.

"But it's fun!" Maya said. "It's like a big adventure."

The younger kids helped by carrying baskets of seeds and watering the freshly planted rows. Even the animals seemed to know something special was happening. Jenny's dog, Oscar, ran happily between the kids, wagging his tail.

By the end of the day, the farm looked much better. The fences were standing tall, the soil was ready for planting, and the barn had a brand-new roof.

Jenny's grandfather clapped his hands together. "I can't believe how much you all did in one day! You kids are amazing."

Jenny beamed. "It's all thanks to Quinn."

Quinn smiled but shook her head. "It's thanks to everyone working together. We helped because we care."

The next week, Jenny's farm had little green sprouts growing where the kids had planted. The farm was alive again! But something even more special happened.

As the kids talked about their day of helping, someone had an idea.

"What if we do this for every farm that needs help?" Emma suggested.

Jack nodded. "Yeah! If another farm gets damaged, we can all go help just like we did for Jenny's."

Jenny's grandfather smiled. "That's the spirit of the countryside. Neighbors helping neighbors."

From that day on, the children in the village made a promise. If any farm needed help, they would all come together—just like they had for Jenny's farm. It became a tradition, passed down to younger kids as they grew up.

And every time a farm was saved, someone would say, “It all started with Quinn.”

What Quinn Learned

Quinn learned that kindness spreads like sunshine. One small act of help can inspire many more. She saw that working together makes even the hardest tasks easier. And most of all, she learned that a little kindness can grow into something bigger than she ever imagined.

Affirmation for Kindness

Write this affirmation in your notebook and say it whenever you want to spread kindness:

“My kindness can make the world a better place.”

Try This

- Do something kind for a friend or neighbor, like helping them carry something or writing them a nice note.
- Ask a grown-up how you can help at home or in your community.
- Think of a way to make someone smile today. It could be as simple as sharing a snack or giving a compliment!

Quinn’s story reminds us that kindness is like planting seeds—it grows into something beautiful. What act of kindness will *you* do today?

Chapter 9: Celine and the Power of Respect

Celine loved family gatherings. They were filled with delicious food, fun games, and lots of laughter. But today, something was different. Today, her parents' friends were visiting, and they had brought their daughter, Nina.

Nina was loud and fast, running through the house like a whirlwind. She grabbed toys without asking, changed the games without warning, and didn't listen when someone said "Stop!"

Celine wasn't sure how to feel. She liked playing with new friends, but she didn't like when people didn't respect her space.

"Mom," Celine whispered as they set the table. "What do I do if someone takes my things without asking?"

Her mother gave her a warm smile. "You set a boundary, sweetheart. If something makes you uncomfortable, you have the right to say 'No.'"

"But what if they get mad?" Celine asked, frowning.

Her mom squeezed her hand. "A real friend will listen. Boundaries show people how to treat you, and when you respect yourself, others will learn to respect you too."

Celine nodded, though she wasn't sure if she was brave enough to do it.

After lunch, Celine and Nina sat on the playroom floor. Celine had her favorite stuffed bunny, Whiskers, cuddled in her lap. She had had Whiskers since she was a baby, and he was very special to her.

"I want that bunny," Nina said, reaching out suddenly.

Celine pulled Whiskers close. "This is my special toy."

"But I want to play with it," Nina insisted. Before Celine could say anything, Nina grabbed Whiskers right out of her hands.

Celine's heart pounded. She felt like she wanted to cry, but then she remembered what her mom had said. *Boundaries show people how to treat you.*

She took a deep breath, stood up tall, and looked Nina in the eyes. "No, Nina. You can't take things without asking. I will share when I'm ready."

Nina blinked, surprised. No one had ever spoken to her like that before.

"But… I always get what I want," Nina mumbled, looking down at the bunny.

Celine shook her head. "That's not fair. You have to ask first. And if someone says no, you have to respect that."

Nina hesitated, then slowly handed Whiskers back. "I'm sorry," she said quietly. "I didn't know that."

Celine softened. "It's okay. We can still play. Do you want to build a castle with blocks?"

Nina's face brightened. "Yes! That sounds fun!"

As they stacked the blocks high, Nina looked over at Celine. "You're really nice, even when you say no."

Celine smiled. "You can say no and still be kind."

Nina thought for a moment. "I guess I never really thought about that. I just take what I want."

Celine shrugged. "Everyone can learn. You can try asking next time."

Nina nodded. "I will. And I'll ask before I touch someone's stuff."

They continued building, laughing as their tower grew taller and taller. When it finally tumbled down, both girls giggled, and Celine knew she had done the right thing.

What Celine Learned

Celine learned that standing up for herself didn't mean being mean—it meant showing others how she wanted to be treated. She realized that saying "no" could be done with kindness and that true friends would listen and learn.

Affirmation for Self-Respect

Write this affirmation in your notebook and say it whenever you need to remind yourself of your worth:

"I respect myself, and I teach others to respect me too."

Try This

- Practice saying "No" in a strong but kind voice. You can try it in front of a mirror!
- Draw a picture of a time when you stood up for yourself. How did it feel?
- Ask a family member about a time they had to set a boundary. What did they learn from it?

Celine's story reminds us that self-respect is important. When we respect ourselves, we show others how to treat us. What boundary will *you* set today?

Part 4: Brave Hearts, Big Adventures

Heya, Courageous Girl!

Have you ever felt scared to try something new? Maybe it was speaking in front of the class, climbing a little higher at the playground, or sleeping with the lights off. Fear can feel big, like a giant shadow, but guess what? You are even bigger and braver than your fears!

Being brave doesn't mean never feeling afraid. It means taking a deep breath and trying anyway. Every time you face a fear, you grow a little stronger, a little wiser, and a lot more confident.

By the time you finish these stories, you'll see that being brave isn't about having no fear—it's about believing in yourself enough to keep going.

So, are you ready to take on your next big adventure? Let's go!

Chapter 10: Adeline and the Lost Moment

Adeline had always lived in a big city, where tall buildings touched the sky and cars honked all day long. But when her father got transferred, everything changed. They moved to a small countryside town, where the air smelled like fresh grass, the roads were quiet, and everyone knew each other's names.

Adeline wasn't sure how she felt about it. The countryside was so different—there were no big toy stores or busy parks like in the city. Instead, there were wide fields, wooden fences, and cows that made funny noises whenever she walked by.

"It's nice here, Adeline," her mother said one morning. "You'll love it once you explore."

Adeline wasn't so sure. But she nodded and smiled anyway.

One afternoon, Adeline and her mother went to the town's little grocery store. Unlike the huge supermarkets she was used to, this store was small and cozy.

There were wooden shelves filled with fresh bread, jars of homemade jam, and baskets of colorful fruits. The store smelled sweet, like cinnamon and apples.

"Why don't you pick some apples while I get the milk?" her mom said.

Adeline nodded and walked to the fruit section. She carefully picked up a bright red apple and turned it over in her hand. It looked delicious! But when she turned back around—her mom was gone!

Her heart started to pound. She looked left, then right. The store suddenly felt much bigger. Her hands felt sweaty, and her chest felt tight. *What if I can't find her? What if I'm lost forever?*

She wanted to run and call for her mom, but then she remembered something her parents had told her before.

"If you ever get lost, don't run. Stay where you are and ask for help."

Adeline took a deep breath and tried to calm her racing heart. *Stay where you are. Ask for help.*

She looked around and saw an older man behind the store counter, smiling kindly at a customer. He had silver hair, round glasses, and a warm face that reminded her of a storybook grandfather. He looked like someone who worked there, someone who could help.

Adeline swallowed hard. Her hands were still shaking, but she knew she had to be brave. She took a deep breath, just like her parents had taught her, and stepped forward.

Summoning all her courage, Adeline walked up to him. "Excuse me," she said, her voice a little wobbly. "I can't find my mom."

The shopkeeper, Mr. Harold, turned and immediately noticed the worry on her face. He knelt down so he was at her eye level, his eyes soft with understanding.

"Oh, don't worry, sweetheart," he said gently. "You're not alone. What's your name?"

"Adeline," she said, gripping the edge of her dress.

"Well, Adeline, your mom must be looking for you too. Let's see if we can find her together," he said, giving her a reassuring pat on the shoulder.

He stood up and looked around. "Now, let's think—where did you last see her?"

Adeline bit her lip. "By the milk section," she said. "But she was getting more things."

Mr. Harold nodded. "Then she might still be nearby. Let's go check the front of the store first."

He led her toward the entrance, walking slowly so she wouldn't feel rushed. Adeline's heart was still thumping, but something about his calm voice made her feel a little steadier. She wasn't alone anymore. She had asked for help, and someone had listened.

A moment later, she heard a familiar voice. "Adeline!"

Her mother rushed over, eyes wide with relief, and scooped her up into a warm hug. "I was so worried! Are you okay?"

Adeline nodded. "I got scared, but then I remembered what you told me. I stayed in one place and asked for help."

Her mom smiled, smoothing Adeline's hair. "I'm so proud of you. You stayed calm and did exactly the right thing."

After they finished shopping, Mr. Harold handed Adeline a small bag of caramel candies. "For being so brave," he said with a wink.

As they walked home, Adeline noticed something she hadn't before. People waved as they passed by. Neighbors smiled and greeted her mom by name. Even Mr. Harold knew who she was.

"Everyone knows each other here," her mom said. "That's what makes the countryside special. If you ever need help, someone will always be there."

Adeline thought about that. Maybe the countryside wasn't so scary after all. Maybe it was actually… kind of nice.

What Adeline Learned

Adeline learned that even when she was scared, she could stay calm and ask for help. She realized that fear didn't have to stop her—she could face it with courage. And most of all, she discovered that the countryside was filled with kind people who looked out for each other.

Affirmation for Bravery

Write this affirmation in your notebook and say it whenever you feel scared:

"I am brave. I can stay calm and find a solution."

Try This

- Think of a time when you were scared. How did you handle it? Talk about it with a friend or family member.
- Practice asking for help in different situations. Who would you go to if you needed help at a store, school, or park?
- Imagine you're lost in a fun place like a theme park or a fair. What would you do first? Talk about your plan with a friend or family member and see what they would do!

Adeline's story reminds us that even when we feel lost, there is always a way to find our way back. Who will *you* help today?

Chapter 11: Elsie and the Thunderstorm Camping Night

Elsie had been waiting for this night for weeks. Her dad had promised her a backyard camping trip, just the two of them, under the wide-open sky. He had even said they would watch the stars, and he would teach her all about space—about twinkling constellations, the glowing moon, and maybe even a shooting star!

She was so excited as they set up the big green tent in the backyard, laying out cozy blankets and pillows inside. Elsie brought her flashlight, her favorite stuffed bunny, and a notebook to write down everything her dad will teach her about the stars.

"This is going to be the best night ever!" she cheered, zipping up the tent.

Her dad chuckled as he helped arrange their sleeping bags. "It sure will be, kiddo."

But just as they were about to step outside and look up at the sky, a loud *BOOM* shook the air.

Elsie jumped, grabbing onto her dad's arm. "What was that?!"

Her dad looked up. Dark clouds had begun rolling in, covering the twinkling stars. Another *CRACK* of thunder rumbled through the sky, and soon, raindrops started falling.

"Oh no!" Elsie cried. "The stars! We won't see them now."

Her dad sighed but smiled reassuringly. "It looks like we have a change of plans, but that doesn't mean the adventure is over."

As the rain got heavier, Elsie felt her heart thudding in her chest. The tent shook slightly from the wind, and the sound of raindrops tapping against it grew louder. She thought about running inside to her cozy bedroom where she'd be safe and warm. *What if the storm gets worse? What if the tent blows away?*

Her dad must have seen the worried look on her face because he said, "Elsie, nature isn't something to be afraid of. It's something to learn from. Let's listen."

Elsie sat still, hugging her bunny tight. She focused on the raindrops. They didn't sound scary. They sounded… soothing, like a soft drumbeat. The thunder wasn't angry—it was just loud, like when her dad clapped his hands really hard.

She took a deep breath and nodded. "Okay… tell me more."

Her dad smiled and pulled out a lantern. "Did you know that thunderstorms help the Earth? They bring rain to help plants grow. And when lightning flashes in the sky, it helps clean the air."

Elsie's eyes widened. "Really?"

"Really," her dad said. "And off-grid campers, like explorers who live in the wild, learn how to stay safe and comfortable even during storms."

He showed her how to make their tent extra secure, tucking in the edges and making sure their gear was dry. He even let her hold the lantern while he explained how people used them before electricity.

Elsie was still disappointed about missing the stars, but now, she felt something else too—curiosity. The storm wasn't ruining their night. It was making it different. Maybe even special.

As the rain continued outside, Elsie and her dad made shadow puppets on the tent wall with their lantern. They laughed as their bunny and butterfly shadows danced.

Then, her dad pulled out a book about space. "Since we can't see the stars, why don't we learn about them anyway?"

Elsie's frown turned into a smile. "Okay!"

They read about planets, meteors, and astronauts. Elsie learned that even astronauts get scared sometimes—but they keep going because they believe in themselves.

When the rain finally slowed to a soft drizzle, Elsie peeked outside. The sky was still cloudy, but the air smelled fresh, and everything looked shiny from the rain.

"This wasn't so scary after all," she admitted.

Her dad gave her a high-five. "See? You faced something new and found the good in it. That's bravery, Elsie."

She beamed. Maybe tonight wasn't what she expected, but she had learned something even more important than just stars—she had learned how to be strong, even when things didn't go as planned.

What Elsie Learned

Elsie learned that not every scary moment is truly scary—sometimes, it's just something new. By staying calm, listening, and learning, she discovered that thunderstorms weren't bad at all. And even though she missed the stars, she gained something even more special: confidence in herself.

Affirmation for Courage

Write this affirmation in your notebook and say it whenever you feel unsure:
"I am brave, I can handle the unexpected, and I can always find the good in every adventure."

Try This

- Next time you hear a thunderstorm, listen carefully. What does it sound like? How does it make you feel?
- Make shadow puppets with a flashlight or lantern and tell a fun story.
- Ask a grown-up about a time they faced something unexpected and how they handled it. What can you learn from their experience?

Elsie's story reminds us that sometimes, the best adventures happen when we least expect them. What will *you* discover the next time things don't go as planned?

Chapter 12: Katarina the Wildlife Protector

Katarina loved animals. She loved the way birds chirped in the morning, the way butterflies danced in the air, and how rabbits twitched their noses when nibbling on grass. But most of all, she loved learning about how every creature played a part in nature.

One weekend, her family visited a wildlife national park, a place filled with nature's wonders. As they rode through the winding paths, Katarina's eyes widened at the sight of elephants walking gracefully, their trunks swaying as they moved. She giggled as she watched playful monkeys swing from tree to tree, chattering excitedly. Brightly colored birds filled the sky, their feathers shimmering in the sunlight as they soared overhead.

As they walked through the park, Katarina's parents pointed out different animals and explained their importance. "Every animal, no matter how big or small, is important," her dad said. "They all have a role in our ecological system."

Her mom knelt beside her and added, "The elephants help shape the land, the birds spread seeds that grow into new trees, and even the tiniest insects help keep nature balanced."

Katarina listened closely, amazed at how everything was connected. She didn't fully understand what *ecological system* meant, but she did understand something even more important—every life mattered, and it was up to humans to help protect animals and nature. She promised herself that one day, she would do something to help the creatures of the world.

One afternoon at school, Katarina and her classmates were playing outside during recess when she heard a strange sound—a soft, high-pitched chirping. It sounded different from the happy songs birds usually sang.

She followed the noise to the edge of the playground near the bushes. That's when she saw it—a small bird, shivering on the ground. Its tiny wing was bent in an odd way, and it looked too weak to fly.

"Oh no!" Katarina gasped.

Her friend, Maren, peeked over her shoulder. "What happened to it?"

"I think it's hurt," Katarina said. "We have to help."

A few kids gathered around, but most of them hesitated.

"You shouldn't touch it," one boy said. "What if it bites you?"

Another girl wrinkled her nose. "Or what if it has germs?"

Katarina took a deep breath. She remembered what her parents had told her at the wildlife park. This bird was small and helpless. It needed care, not fear.

She looked at her friends and said, "If we were hurt, wouldn't we want someone to help us?"

Maren nodded. "That's true."

Katarina gently took off her sweater and carefully wrapped it around the tiny bird.

"It's okay, little one," she whispered. "We're going to help you."

Holding the bird close to her chest, Katarina walked toward the school building. Her heart pounded. What if the teacher didn't know what to do? What if the bird didn't make it?

But she pushed those thoughts away. *One step at a time*, she told herself. She had to try.

She found her teacher, Miss Rose, who immediately saw the concern in Katarina's eyes.

"Miss Rose, we found a hurt bird," Katarina explained. "Can we help it?"

Miss Rose smiled gently. "That was very brave of you, Katarina. Let's take it to the nurse's office and see what we can do."

The school nurse, Mrs. Bennett, found a small box and lined it with soft tissues. Katarina carefully placed the bird inside, making sure it was comfortable.

Mrs. Bennett called the local wildlife rescue center. "They'll be here soon to take care of the bird," she said. "You did the right thing, Katarina."

Katarina felt a warm glow inside her. She looked down at the bird and smiled. It was still weak, but now it had a chance.

"You're going to be okay," she whispered.

At lunch, Maren sat next to Katarina. "You were really brave today," she said. "I didn't know what to do, but you did."

Katarina shrugged. "I just remembered what my parents told me—every life matters."

By the end of the day, the whole class had heard about Katarina and the little bird. Some kids who had been too scared to help before now asked questions about animals and nature. Miss Rose even decided to add a lesson about protecting wildlife in their next science class.

When Katarina got home, she told her parents everything. They hugged her tightly. “You made a difference today,” her mom said. “That bird got a second chance because of you.”

Katarina smiled. She realized something important—not all heroes wore capes. Some wore school sweaters and had gentle hands. And some, like her, just needed the courage to take action.

What Katarina Learned

Katarina learned that being brave doesn’t mean not being scared—it means doing what’s right even when others hesitate. She saw how one small act of kindness could make a big impact and inspire others. Most of all, she realized that every creature, no matter how tiny, is part of our world and deserves care.

Affirmation for Protecting Nature

Write this affirmation in your notebook and say it whenever you want to remind yourself of your power to help:

“Every life matters, and I can make a difference.”

Try This

- Draw a picture of your favorite animal and write one way you can help protect it.
- Go outside and listen to the sounds of nature. What birds or animals do you hear?
- Talk to a family member about how you can help take care of the environment, like planting flowers for bees or picking up litter in your neighborhood.

Katarina's story reminds us that even the smallest actions can create big changes.

How will *you* help nature today?

Part 5: The Power of a Thankful Heart

Heya, Sunshine!

Have you ever felt really happy when someone gave you a big hug or shared something special with you? That warm, fuzzy feeling inside? That's gratitude! It's like a little bit of magic that makes everything feel brighter.

Being thankful isn't just about saying "thank you." It's about noticing the good things around you—your family, your friends, the fun moments, and even the little things, like a sunny day or a kind smile. The more you practice gratitude, the happier and stronger you feel!

By the time you finish these stories, you'll see that a thankful heart is a happy heart, and happiness makes you shine even brighter!

So, are you ready to discover the magic of gratitude? Let's begin!

Chapter 13: Audrey and the Uncomfortable Tickling

Audrey loved playing outside with her friends. Every afternoon, after school, she and the neighborhood kids would gather at the playground. Her favorite part was swinging high up in the air, feeling the wind rush through her hair. But there was one thing that made her a little uncomfortable—her friend Liam's tickling.

Liam was always playful. He liked to make everyone laugh, and his favorite way to do that was by tickling. Whenever Audrey was on the swings, he would run up behind her and tickle her sides, making her squeal and jump. The other kids would giggle, thinking it was funny. But Audrey didn't think so.

She didn't like the way it made her feel or how she couldn't focus on swinging. It made her feel out of control, and even though Liam wasn't trying to be mean, it didn't feel good.

One evening, Audrey sat with her mom at the dinner table. She hesitated before speaking but finally said, "Mom, I don't like it when Liam tickles me at the playground."

Her mom put down her fork and gave Audrey her full attention. "Oh, sweetheart, I'm glad you told me. What happens when he tickles you?"

Audrey sighed. "I don't like the feeling. It makes me feel weird, and I want him to stop, but I don't know how to say it."

Her mom nodded. "That's because your body is telling you something very important, Audrey. You have the right to say no to any touch that makes you uncomfortable. Your body belongs to you, and no one should touch you in a way that you don't like."

Audrey listened carefully. "But what if I hurt his feelings?"

Her mom smiled gently. "Being kind to others is important, but it's also important to be kind to yourself. You can tell Liam how you feel in a firm but polite way. If he is a good friend, he will understand."

Audrey thought about this for a moment. She had never said no to Liam before. But maybe she should try.

The next day at the playground, Audrey climbed onto the swing as usual. Liam ran up behind her, ready to tickle her again. But this time, before he could, Audrey took a deep breath and turned to face him.

"Liam, stop," she said firmly. "I don't like being tickled. Please don't do it again."

Liam blinked in surprise. "You don't like it?"

Audrey shook her head. "No, it makes me feel uncomfortable. My mom said I have the right to say no if I don't like how something feels."

Liam looked thoughtful. "I didn't know that. I thought it was just a game."

"It might be fun for you, but it's not fun for me," Audrey explained.

Liam hesitated, then nodded. "Okay, I won't do it anymore."

Audrey felt a huge weight lift off her chest. She had spoken up, and Liam had listened.

For the rest of the afternoon, Audrey played happily. She swung high into the air without worrying about being tickled. When she got home, she ran to her mom and hugged her tightly.

"Mom! It worked! I told Liam to stop, and he listened!"

Her mom smiled proudly. "I knew you could do it. How do you feel?"

Audrey grinned. "Happy. And safe."

Her mom kissed her forehead. "That's because you respected yourself, and Liam respected you too. You have the right to set boundaries, and when you do, you feel better."

Audrey realized something important that day—what her mom had taught her wasn't just words. It was something real, something that could help her feel safe and happy. And for that, she was truly grateful.

What Audrey Learned

Audrey learned that she has the right to say no to any touch that makes her uncomfortable. She realized that speaking up for herself didn't mean being mean—it meant taking care of her own feelings. And best of all, she saw that good friends will respect boundaries when they understand them.

Affirmation for Feeling Safe and Strong

Write this affirmation in your notebook and say it whenever you need to remind yourself of your rights:

"I am grateful for my body and my feelings. I have the right to say no to anything that makes me uncomfortable, and I am proud of myself for speaking up."

Try This

- Play the 'Superhero Boundaries' game! Pretend you are a superhero with a special shield that protects you from things you don't like. Practice saying 'No, stop!' in a strong voice while holding up your imaginary shield.
- Create a kindness and respect poster with your friend! Draw or write about different ways people can respect each other's personal space and feelings, and share it with your family.
- Talk to a family member about personal space and body boundaries. What do they think is important about respecting others?

Audrey's story reminds us that everyone deserves to feel safe. What will *you* do to stand up for yourself today?

Chapter 14: Fiona and the Worn-Out Shoes

Fiona loved her pink sneakers. They had tiny stars on the sides and sparkly laces that shimmered in the sunlight. But lately, her sneakers weren't as bright as before. The soles were scuffed, the stars had faded, and the sparkles on the laces had almost disappeared.

One morning, as she put them on for school, she sighed. "I wish I had new shoes," she mumbled.

Her mom smiled. "They still fit you and keep your feet safe, don't they?"

Fiona nodded but didn't feel any better. When she got to school, she saw her friend Aria wearing brand-new purple sneakers with flashing lights on the sides. When Aria walked, her shoes blinked in red, blue, and green.

"Wow," Fiona whispered. "Those are so cool."

Aria grinned. "I just got them yesterday! They even make a sound when I jump!" She hopped up, and her sneakers let out a tiny *beep!*

Fiona looked down at her own shoes. They looked even older compared to Aria's. She crossed her feet, hoping no one would notice them.

During recess, Fiona sat on the bench, watching other kids play. She was still thinking about Aria's sneakers when she noticed a boy sitting alone near the swings. His shoes caught her attention—they had holes in them. The soles were almost gone, and his socks peeked out through the torn fabric. Every time he moved, little bits of dirt got into his shoes.

Fiona's heart sank. *His shoes are much older than mine,* she thought. *And they don't even protect his feet.*

She watched as the boy stood up and carefully walked across the playground, trying not to step on anything sharp. He wasn't complaining. He wasn't even looking at anyone else's shoes. He was just happy to play.

Suddenly, Fiona felt something different inside her. She looked down at her own sneakers again, but this time, she didn't feel sad. *My shoes may not be new, but they still work. They keep my feet safe, and I can run and jump without worrying about getting hurt.*

That evening at dinner, Fiona told her parents about the boy at school. "His shoes had big holes in them," she said. "I felt bad for complaining about mine."

Her dad nodded. "It's okay to want nice things, Fiona. But sometimes, when we see what others don't have, we realize how lucky we are."

Fiona thought for a moment. Then she asked, "Can we help kids like him?"

Her mom smiled proudly. "That's a wonderful idea. How do you think we can help?"

Fiona's eyes lit up. "Maybe we can give away shoes we don't need anymore! Maybe other kids at school can help too!"

Her parents loved the idea. Over the weekend, Fiona and her mom went through her closet and found two pairs of sneakers she had outgrown. They packed them into a box and brought them to a donation center.

On Monday, Fiona felt different when she put on her sneakers. Although they were still old, but now she felt grateful for them. When she saw the boy again, she smiled at him.

"Hi, I'm Fiona."

He looked up, surprised. "I'm Lucas."

They talked for a while, and Fiona learned that Lucas had just moved to their town. His family was still settling in, and he hadn't gotten a chance to get anything new yet.

Fiona felt warm inside. *Helping others feels even better than getting something new.*

What Fiona Learned

Fiona learned that it's okay to want nice things, but it's even more important to be grateful for what you already have. She realized that there are always people who have less, and a little kindness can make a big difference. Most of all, she discovered that helping others feels even better than getting something new.

Affirmation for Gratitude

Write this affirmation in your notebook and say it whenever you feel like comparing what you have to others:

"I am thankful for what I have, and I can use what I have to help others."

Try This

- Create a gratitude tree! Draw a big tree on paper and cut out paper leaves. Every day, write one thing you're thankful for on a leaf and stick it to the tree. Watch your tree grow with all the wonderful things in your life!
- Talk about gratitude with your family at dinner. Take turns saying one thing you're thankful for that day.
- Think of a way to help someone who might need extra kindness, like donating toys, clothes, or even just writing a kind note to a friend.

Fiona's story reminds us that gratitude can change the way we see the world. What are *you* grateful for today?

Chapter 15: Marigold and the Broken Toy

Marigold had one favorite toy in the whole wide world—her beloved doll, Rosie. Rosie wasn't just any doll. She had golden yarn hair, a soft pink dress with tiny flowers, and bright blue eyes that never faded, no matter how much Marigold hugged her.

Rosie had been with Marigold for as long as she could remember. She had been there for tea parties, bedtime stories, long car rides, and even the big move from the city to the countryside.

Life in the countryside was different from the city. There weren't big toy stores or shops on every corner. If something broke, people didn't just rush to buy a new one—they fixed what they could and cherished what they had. But Marigold hadn't thought much about that. Not until one sunny afternoon did everything change.

That day, Marigold was playing in the barn, setting up a pretend tea party for Rosie and her stuffed animals. She carefully placed Rosie on a wooden crate while she fetched some imaginary tea.

Just as she reached for her toy teapot, a strong gust of wind blew through the open barn doors. *WHOOSH!* The crate wobbled, and Rosie tumbled off, landing with a loud *CRACK* on the barn floor.

Marigold gasped and rushed over. She picked Rosie up, hoping she was okay—but her heart sank. Rosie's arm had snapped right off.

Tears welled in Marigold's eyes. "No, no, no!" she whispered, holding the tiny broken arm in her hands. She tried to push it back in place, but it wobbled and fell off again.

She wanted to run inside and tell her parents. In the city, they would have gone to a store and gotten a new doll instantly. But here, things were different. Things took time.

Her dad had once told her that i*n the countryside, we fix what we can and cherish what we have.*

Marigold sniffled, hugged Rosie close, and walked toward the house.

Her father was sitting on the porch, fixing a broken wooden chair. When he saw Marigold's sad face, he set down his tools. "What's wrong, dear?"

Marigold held up Rosie. "She's broken, Dad."

Her father took a deep breath, gently turning the doll over in his hands. "Oh, I see. Rosie's been with you for a long time, hasn't she?"

Marigold nodded, her lower lip trembling. "I love her so much. But now she's broken, and I can't fix her."

Her dad patted the wooden porch beside him. "Come sit, Marigold. Let me tell you something about life in the countryside."

She climbed up next to him, still holding Rosie tightly.
"You know," her dad said, "out here in the countryside, I told you that we don't throw things away just because they're a little broken. I also mentioned that in life, we need to fix what we can and cherish the things that have been with us for a long time. But more than that, we remember the good times we had with them."
Marigold blinked. "But Rosie can't be fixed."
Her dad nodded. "Maybe not, but that doesn't mean she stops being special. Think of all the adventures you've had with her. All the tea parties, all the bedtime stories, all the hugs."
Marigold thought about it. Rosie had been there through everything. Even if she was missing an arm, she was still the same Rosie.
Her dad smiled. "Memories are what make something truly valuable, not just how perfect it looks. We always hold onto the things that bring us joy, even if they're not brand new anymore."
Marigold looked down at Rosie. She thought about all the happy moments they had shared. And suddenly, instead of feeling sad, she started to feel… grateful.
"You know what, Dad?" Marigold said, standing up. "I think I want to keep Rosie just the way she is. She's still my best doll, even with one arm."
Her dad chuckled. "That's my girl. You've got the heart of a true kid."
That night, Marigold found a special place for Rosie on her shelf, right next to her favorite bedtime books. Every time she looked at her, she felt happy remembering all the fun they had together.
Marigold beamed. She felt warm inside—not because she still had Rosie, but because she realized that Rosie had taught her an important lesson—memories matter more than things, and gratitude can make even broken moments beautiful.

What Marigold Learned

Marigold learned that being grateful for memories is more important than having perfect things. She also discovered that gratitude could turn sadness into happiness.

Affirmation for Cherishing Memories

Write this affirmation in your journal and say it when you feel sad about losing something special:

"I am grateful for the memories I make. Even when things change, the love and joy I felt will always stay with me."

Try This

- Find a small box and fill it with little things that remind you of happy times, such as a drawing, a ticket stub, or a photo. Whenever you miss something, look inside!
- Write down something you are grateful for on a small slip of paper and add it to a paper chain. Add a new one each day and watch your gratitude chain grow!
- Tell a friend or family member about an item that's important to you. Why do you love it? What memories do you have with it?

Marigold's story reminds us that things may not last forever, but our love and gratitude can stay in our hearts forever. What memories are *you* grateful for today?

Your Beautiful Journey Ahead

Heya, Wonderful Girl!

Look how far you've come! You've learned about bravery, confidence, friendship, facing fears, and the power of gratitude. But guess what? This is just the beginning of your journey!

Every day is a new adventure, and every challenge is a chance to grow. You won't always have all the answers, and that's okay. What truly matters is that you keep going, keep believing in yourself, and keep shining as the wonderful, kind, and brave girl you are.

Let's take a moment to remember all the incredible things you've discovered:

- **Courage** helps you take the first step, even when things feel scary.
- **Confidence** isn't about being the best—it's about believing in yourself.
- **Friendship and kindness** make life brighter and more meaningful.
- **Facing your fears** makes you stronger and helps you discover new strengths.
- **Gratitude** turns little moments into big joys and makes your heart feel full.

And most importantly—you are already enough, just as you are. ☺

So, what's next for you? A new dream? A big adventure? A small, brave step forward? Whatever it is, you have everything inside you to make it happen.

Go out there and shine, my wonderful sweet little girl—the world is waiting for you!

With love and belief in you…

Your Biggest Cheerleader

Sati… ✍

Thank You

Hey there, Wonderful Girl!

Wow, you made it to the end of the book—high five! I'm so proud of you for going on this journey with me. I hope you had fun, learned new things, and feel ready to conquer the world!

Thank you so much for reading this book and sharing this journey with me. Now, I need your help. Could you ask your grown-up to leave a review for this book? It's super easy and helps me write more stories like this for you and other amazing girls. Just give them a nudge (like, "Please!") and let them know how much you loved it.

Scan Me

>> Leave a Review on Amazon<<

Thank you for being so awesome—you're my best wonder-girl!

BOOKS BY SATI SIRODA

Mind the Quote

Poulomi's Abode of Thoughts

Coffee Tales: Short Stories of Wisdom

Earnest Poetica: Ink Expressions of the Ineffable Heart

Gratitude Journal: Reflect, Appreciate, Transform in 60 Days

Inspiring Stories for Amazing Girls Who Believe in Themselves

Inspiring Stories for Amazing Boys Who Believe in Themselves

I am 6 and Brave

Whispers of the Zen Forest

Whispers of the Zen Forest Workbook

Mastering Herbal Synergies

About the Author

Sati Siroda crafts narratives that transcend age, speaking to the universal human spirit. Drawing from a multifaceted background in engineering, education, business, and communication, Sati crafts stories that resonate across generations and speak to a deep, holistic understanding of the mind.

The Art of the Meaningful Pattern

Sati's signature style is defined by intentional simplicity. She writes in clear, accessible English, placing profound weight on every word. Her work utilizes rhythmic patterns—a deliberate technique designed to mirror how the human brain processes and retains wisdom for longer. This intentional cadence ensures her message of courage and self-discovery is not just read, but deeply felt—almost as if it were a manifestation that takes root in the reader's consciousness.

A Holistic Approach to Growth

Sati explores a vast range of genres, from fiction to insightful non-fiction. Regardless of the form her writing takes, an "inspirational angle" remains her north star, ensuring that every book serves as a catalyst for personal evolution.

- Universal Reach: Her books serve as tools for anyone seeking resilience and self-love, regardless of their age or background.
- Structured Insight: She leverages her multifaceted expertise to create "stepping stone" narratives that make emotional growth feel intuitive.
- The Mission: Every word written is designed to foster growth, helping readers navigate life's challenges with creativity, optimism, and a clear sense of purpose.

Through the enchantment of her books, Sati invites everyone to embark on a journey of self-discovery, proving that the right words, arranged in the right patterns, can unlock the potential within us all.

Stay connected with Sati Siroda on Instagram: *@SatiSiroda.*

www.ingramcontent.com/pod-product-compliance
Lightning Source LLC
Chambersburg PA
CBHW062144160726
48282CB00027B/941
* 9 7 8 8 1 9 8 5 3 3 7 0 8 *